Ruth Owen

In the Amazon rainforest

CLASH

Publisher: Melissa Fairley
Art Director: Faith Booker
Editor: Emma Dods
Designer: Emma Randall
Production Controller: Ed Green
Production Manager: Suzy Kelly

ISBN: 978 1 84898 212 3

Copyright © *TickTock* Entertainment Ltd 2010
First published in Great Britain in 2010 by *TickTock* Entertainment Ltd,
The Old Sawmill, 103 Goods Station Road, Tunbridge Wells, Kent, TN1 2DP

Printed in China
1 3 5 7 9 10 8 6 4 2

Picture credits (t=top; b=bottom; c=centre; l=left; r=right; OFC=outside front cover; OBC=outside back cover):
Arco Images GmbH/Alamy: 20–21. John Clegg/ardea.com: 7b. Michael Doolittle/Alamy: 19. Eye Ubiquitous/Alamy: 29b.
John Giustina/Getty Images: 15. Monalyn Gracia/Corbis: 8t. iStock: 2, 12tr, 12c, 12b, 14, 18bl, 22, 28t, 31cr. Wolfgang
Kaehler/Corbis: 6b. Robb Kendrick/Getty Images: 18bc. Gerd Ludwig/Corbis: 6t. NHPA/Bill Love: 21b. NHPA/Mark
Bowler: 10t. Photo 24/Getty Images: 23. Photodisc/Getty Images: 26–27. Paul Raffaele/Rex Features: 29t. Shutterstock:
OFC, 1, 4, 5, 7t, 7c, 8b (both), 9, 11t, 11c, 12tl, 13 (both), 16–17 (all), 18t, 18br, 24, 25, 28b, 31t (x 3), 31cl, 3c, OBC.
www.janespencer.com: 9t, 10b, 11b.

Thank you to Lorraine Petersen and the members of nasen.

Every effort has been made to trace copyright holders, and we apologize in advance for any omissions.
We would be pleased to insert the appropriate acknowledgements in any subsequent edition of this publication.

NOTE TO READERS
The website addresses are correct at the time of publishing. However, due to the ever-changing
nature of the Internet, websites and content may change. Some websites can contain links that
are unsuitable for children. The publisher is not responsible for changes in content or website
addresses. We advise that Internet searches should be supervised by an adult.

Neither the publishers nor the author shall be liable for any bodily harm or damage to property whatsoever
that may be caused or sustained as a result of conducting any of the activities featured in this book.

A Jaguar

CHAPTER 1

LOST IN THE JUNGLE

In your everyday life you have everything you need to survive.

Food comes from a shop.

Water comes from a tap.

Your home is warm, dry and safe.

You don't have to think about survival.

So, what would happen if one day all that changed? What would happen if you were flying over a jungle and your plane crashed?

Would you know how to survive...

...in a jungle?

The Amazon rainforest is a huge jungle in South America.

5.5 million square kilometres of rainforest

In the rainforest, heavy rain falls non-stop for days. You can collect rainwater for drinking in large leaves.

Millions of insects and other animals live in the rainforest. So, you will have plenty to eat!

Army ant carrying a larva

Termite nest

Look under logs for termites, ants and their larvae.

Look in jungle streams for shrimp.

Shrimp

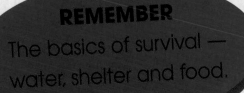
REMEMBER
The basics of survival — water, shelter and food.

CHAPTER 2

SHELTER

**To stay alive, you must build a shelter.
A shelter will protect you from the rain.**

You will need tools to build a shelter. If you have
no equipment, you must improvise. This means you
must think of new ways to do things.

- A metal belt buckle
  can become a knife.

- A large rock can be
  used as a hammer.

Plant stems can be shredded to make fibres.
Fibres can be twisted together to make string or rope.

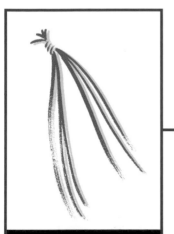

Secure the stems
with a knot.

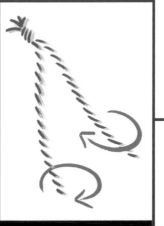

Twist both strands
clockwise.

Twist one strand
around the other.

Stem

9

You will need to find a place to build your shelter.
Find a place that's higher than any nearby rivers.
A sudden flood could wash away your shelter.

Rain in the Amazon rainforest

Everything you need to build your shelter will be around you.

Cover the shelter in large leaves.

Tie branches to trees with string made from plant fibres.

Imagine waking up to find a million army ants marching through your shelter. You wouldn't want to be sleeping on the ground!

Army ants hunt in huge colonies. They will eat 50,000 other insects in a day.

Army ants

A raised bed will stop insects, scorpions and snakes climbing over you during the night.

Cover the bed in leaves and grass.

CHAPTER 3

FIRE

**You need a fire for cooking and warmth.
When the rain stops, look for a clearing.
Here, the hot sun will soon dry out materials.**

To build a fire you need tinder, kindling and fuel.

Tinder is material that
will catch alight easily.

*Use dry moss or bird
feathers for tinder.*

*Use dry leaves
for kindling.*

Then you add kindling,
which helps the fire
to burn strongly.

*Use bark or broken
branches for fuel.*

Then you add fuel, which
will burn for a long time.

If you have no matches, you will need to make a spark.

Look on the river bank for flint or a sharp-edged rock. Strike the flint with a carbon steel knife. The knife will make a spark.

Don't let your fire go out. At night, cover the fire with hot ashes. If you stop air getting to the fire, it will burn very slowly.

In the morning, when you brush away the ashes, the fire will still be burning.

At night, a fire will also protect you...

**...from the jaguar.
You won't see him.
But he could be
nearby. Watching YOU.**

The jaguar is the world's third largest big cat
after the tiger and lion. A male jaguar can
be nearly two metres long including its tail.

CHAPTER 4

FINDING FOOD

You need food for energy. Food also helps to raise your morale. This means it makes you feel more able to cope with your situation.

Ant

Beetle

Cricket

Termite

Crush ants, beetles, crickets and termites together to make a tasty paste.

Dig for earthworms in the leaves and soil.

Eat them raw.

Earthworms

Look for birds' nests. Take one or two eggs to eat. Mark the other eggs with charcoal from your fire.

When you go back to a nest, any eggs without the mark will be freshly laid.

Charcoal

Frog

Never eat jungle frogs or mushrooms – many are poisonous.

There are many streams and rivers in the Amazon. All freshwater fish are safe to eat. Always boil them or roast them on your fire.

You could make a fishing spear. Sharpen a stem of bamboo to make a spear. Stand still in shallow water with the spear point underwater.

Move the point slowly towards a fish. Then, with a sudden push, pin the fish to the river bed.

Bamboo

To make a fishing rod you can improvise. Use your bootlaces as a fishing line. A thorn from a plant can be used as a hook. A worm can be used as bait.

Bootlaces

Thorn

Worms

Spear fishing from a canoe

CHAPTER 5

JUNGLE DANGERS

Many dangerous animals live in the Amazon...
...and you are on their territory!

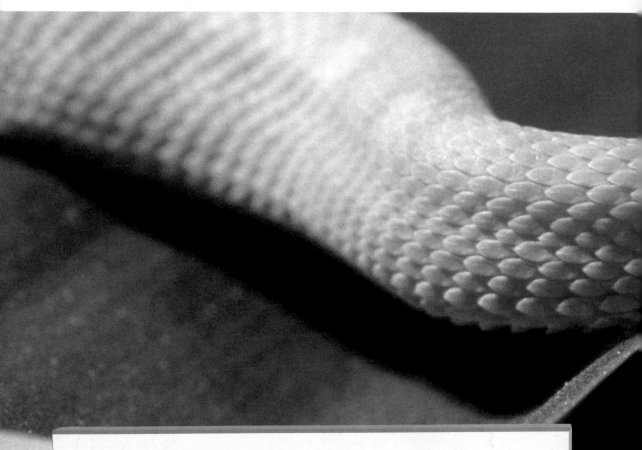

To avoid snakebites, follow these rules:
- Don't step over logs. Step up onto a log, check below, then step down.
- Use a stick to turn over logs and rocks.
- Use a long stick to push aside branches.
- Watch for snakes when picking fruit.

The eyelash pit viper hunts frogs and birds in low-hanging branches. It will sometimes attack even if you have not disturbed it.

Its venomous bite can cause severe body tissue damage.

Eyelash pit viper

The green anaconda is the world's largest snake. It can grow up to ten metres long.

It waits in water to catch prey such as deer. It wraps its body around its prey to squeeze out all the air. Then it swallows its prey whole – head first.

Green anaconda

The black caiman is the Amazon's largest water predator. It can grow up to six metres long.

Black caiman

The goliath bird-eating tarantula can have a leg span of 25 centimetres. If it thinks it is in danger, it shoots out tiny hairs. The hairs can irritate your skin and eyes.

Goliath bird-eating tarantula

CHAPTER 6

PROTECT YOUR BODY

It is very important to stay clean in a survival situation. Dirty skin can become infected and cause illness.

Check for things living on your body every day!

Ticks can attach to your body and suck blood. Cover a tick in tree sap. This will cut off the air and the tick will die.

Tick

Leeches also stick to your body and suck blood.

Be careful not to swallow a leech. It could attach to the inside of your throat. Pull off leeches as soon as you can.

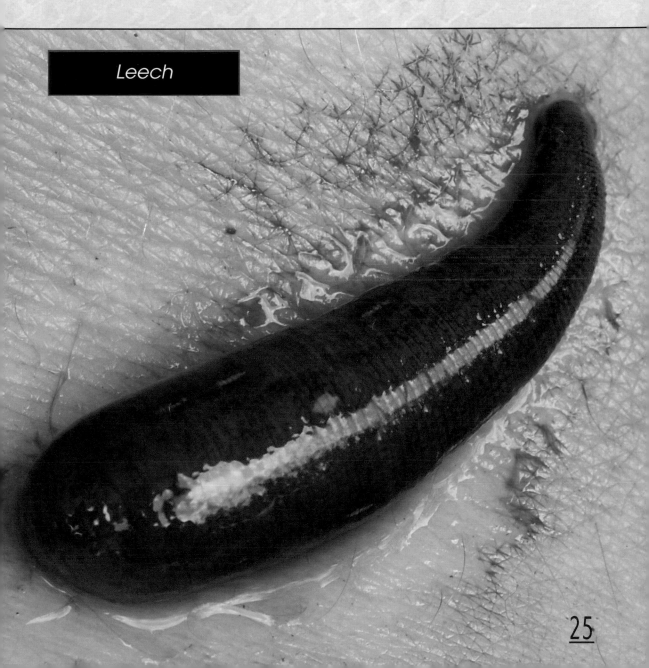

Leech

CHAPTER 7

RESCUE

The jungle is a thick tangle of trees and bushes. This makes it hard for rescue planes to see you.

You can make a signalling mirror. Anything shiny will catch sunlight and create a flash.

You can even use your belt buckle. Always carry it with you in case you hear a plane.

CHAPTER 8

THE SURVIVAL EXPERTS

The Waorani people live in the Amazon in Ecuador. They are experts at jungle survival.

They use blowpipes
and poison darts
to shoot monkeys
for meat.

They add plant
poison to river
water to stun fish.
Then they can catch
the fish by hand.

The Waorani move from place to place. When they move, they carry their fire in a termite nest. This keeps it alight.

Waorani man

Blowpipe

NEED TO KNOW WORDS

camouflage
When something is hidden or blends into the background. An animal can have a fur pattern or skin colour that camouflages it against a background.

clearing An open area where no trees are growing.

colony A large group of animals or people.

improvise To find a new way to do something using only the materials or items you have with you and not the proper tools for the job.

larva A young of many insects, including ants and termites. Larvae hatch from eggs.

morale The way a person or group of people feels about themselves and their abilities.

predator An animal that hunts, kills and eats other animals.

prey An animal that is hunted and killed by another animal for food.

sap A watery, sometimes sticky, liquid inside plants.

span The measurement of something, from end to end.

storey One level, or floor, in a building.

territory In the animal world, a territory is an area of land where an animal lives, finds its food and mates.

traditional Describes something that a group of people have been doing for a long time. The traditional way of doing something is passed on by a person to their children. They then pass it on to their children and so on.

venomous Describes an animal that uses venom to kill its prey or to defend itself. Venom is a poison that is deliberately passed onto a victim through a bite or sting.

THE SURVIVAL KIT

When you are in a survival situation, it's good to improvise. However, it's better to be prepared. Here are some items that would be good to include in your survival kit:

Knife

Compass – a tool that tells you which direction you are heading in.

Whistle to attract rescuers

Matches in a waterproof box

Torch

First aid kit

Always remember to take lots of water.

SURVIVAL ONLINE

A page of websites filled with rainforest facts
www.rain-tree.com/schoolreports.htm

Join film crews, explorers and scientists in the Amazon rainforest.
www.bbc.co.uk/sn/tvradio/programmes/amazon/index.shtml

More tips and information on jungle survival
www.storm-crow.co.uk/articles/jungle_survival.html

INDEX